ACTION SPORTS

FORMULA ONE
CAR RACING

Joe Herran and Ron Thomas

CHELSEA HOUSE
PUBLISHERS
A Haights Cross Communications Company
Philadelphia

This edition first published in 2003 in the United States of America by Chelsea House Publishers, a subsidiary of Haights Cross Communications.

Chelsea House Publishers
1974 Sproul Road, Suite 400
Broomall, PA 19008-0914

The Chelsea House world wide web address is www.chelseahouse.com

Library of Congress Cataloging-in-Publication Data
Herran, Joe.
  Formula One car racing / by Joe Herran and Ron Thomas.
  v. cm. — (Action sports)
  Includes index.
  Contents: What is Formula One car racing? — Formula One gear — Skills, tricks, and techniques — The Formula One racing scene — Racing safely — Grand Prix racing — Grand Prix champions — Then and now — Related action sports.
  ISBN 0-7910-7000-X
  1. Grand Prix racing—Juvenile literature. 2. Formula One automobiles—Juvenile literature.
  [1. Automobile racing. 2. Grand Prix racing. 3. Formula One automobiles.] I. Title: Formula 1 racing.
  II. Thomas, Ron, 1947- III. Title. IV. Action sports (Chelsea House Publishers)
  GV1029.13 .H47 2003
  796.72—dc21
                                                                              2002002293

First published in 2002 by
MACMILLAN EDUCATION AUSTRALIA PTY LTD
627 Chapel Street, South Yarra, Australia, 3141

Edited by Miriana Dasovic
Text design by Karen Young
Cover design by Karen Young
Illustrations by Nives Porcellato and Andy Craig
Page layout by Raul Diche
Photo research by Legend Images

Printed in China

Acknowledgements
Cover photo: Formula One race, courtesy of Sport the library.

AAP/AFP Photo/Paul Crock, p. 13 (bottom); AAP/AP photo/MTI-Sandor H. Szabo, p. 24; Australian Picture Library/Corbis, p. 20; Australian Picture Library/Empics, pp. 9 (bottom), 11 (top), 12, 14, 15, 19 (top), 21, 23 (bottom), 25 (bottom), 29 (left), 30; Daimler Chrysler, pp. 4, 5, 7 (top), 8, 23 (top), 26 (right), 27 (left); Ferrari, p. 25 (top); Getty Images/Allsport, pp. 6–7 (bottom), 10, 11 (bottom), 13 (top), 16, 18, 19 (center), 28 (right), 29 (right); Getty Images/Hulton, pp. 28 (left and center); Sport the library, pp. 9 (top), 17, 19 (bottom), 26 (left), 27 (right).

While every care has been taken to trace and acknowledge copyright the publisher tenders their apologies for any accidental infringement where copyright has proved untraceable.

CONTENTS

Introduction   4

What is Formula One car racing?   5

Formula One gear   6

Skills, tricks and techniques   12

The Formula One racing scene   14

Racing safely   18

Grand Prix racing   22

Grand Prix champions   26

Then and now   28

Related action sports   30

Glossary   31

Index   32

INTRODUCTION

In this book you will read about:
- the formula to which these super cars are built and tested
- the teams that build and maintain the cars
- the drivers and the safety gear they wear
- the rules to protect drivers, mechanics and spectators
- the work of the pit team
- how a Formula One Grand Prix event is staged
- the role of the safety car
- driving strategies
- some leading drivers
- the history of Grand Prix motor racing.

In the beginning

The first car race was held on a road in France in 1894. Soon after, city-to-city car races were being held all over Europe.

Because of the danger to the public caused by these races, special racing **circuits** were built on closed-off roads. The first Grand Prix was held on one such road in 1906. Racing cars improved greatly during the 1930s, and names such as Alfa Romeo and Mercedes-Benz became associated with the sport of motor racing. Formula One – the special formula for cars and the rules for racing them – was devised in 1950.

Formula One racing today

Formula One car racing is a spectacular and fast-moving sport enjoyed by millions of spectators worldwide who watch live at the circuit and on television. Using advanced technology, teams of engineers, highly skilled drivers, mechanics and designers work to build cars to compete in Formula One events held around the world in 17 countries.

WHAT IS FORMULA ONE CAR
RACING?

Formula One car racing involves specially designed cars competing on purpose-built circuits or closed-off roads. 'Grand Prix' is the name given to races that are part of the Formula One World Championship.

A Formula One racing car is a car that has been designed and built to meet the technical requirements of the Federation Internationale de l'Automobile (FIA).

What does the formula say?

The FIA Formula One says that cars must:

- weigh at least 1,322 pounds (600 kilograms), including the weight of the driver and the driver's equipment, and be no wider than 70.86 inches (180 centimeters)
- have a four-stroke engine with no more than 12 cylinders
- have an engine of no more than 3000 cc capacity
- have wheel cables attached to all wheels
- have two separate brake systems so that if one fails, the other will still operate
- be fitted with a built-in fire-extinguishing system
- be fitted with at least two television cameras
- carry an accident data recorder.

Other sections of the formula contain regulations about:

- engine design
- a car's body work, including built-in safety structures
- aerodynamics
- fuel tanks
- refueling
- electrical and cooling systems
- gears
- wheels and tires
- the steering system.

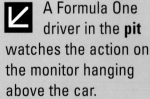
A Formula One driver in the **pit** watches the action on the monitor hanging above the car.

FORMULA ONE
GEAR

↘ ACTION FACT

A Formula One car is made of more than 12,000 different parts.

The car

Formula One cars are constructed by engineers, mechanics and designers with help from drivers. These people are known as the team. The team builds three complete cars for each Grand Prix event.

Building a Formula One car

Designers create a computer model of the car before building a scale model, complete with an engine. This is then tested in a wind tunnel to see what effect the wind will have on the movement and speed of the car. After the tests, changes can be made to the design and any of the parts can be altered or rebuilt.

A full-scale model in wood and paper is made for the engineers to work on. Then a full-scale **chassis** is custom-built for a particular driver. Pedals, seat, headrest, steering wheel and controls are matched to the driver's body. The chassis is then tested for safety in crash tests.

↗ Each part of a Formula One car has to be designed, built and tested separately before it is fitted into the car.

West McLaren Mercedes

The paint used on McLaren-Mercedes cars contains a special ingredient to stop the color fading in the sun.

ACTION FACT

Formula One cars are built low to the ground.

Mechanics then construct the first of the cars that will be used at the Grand Prix. Wheels, tires, **aerofoil wings**, the gearbox and all the other parts are assembled, and the car is painted in the team colors. After thousands of hours of work, the finished car is ready for testing on the track before other cars are built for the Grand Prix season.

If a team uses an engine made by someone else, the engine-maker's name must appear in the team name. The first part of the team name is always that of the constructor of the chassis. The name of the engine maker is second. For example, the name McLaren–Mercedes-Benz tells you that the McLaren team built the chassis and Mercedes provided the engine.

At the end of each Formula One Grand Prix, a **Constructor's Cup** is awarded to the maker of the winning car.

The engine

The heart of a Formula One car is the engine. The engine is the machine that burns fuel to produce the power that moves the car. Design engineers aim to build an engine that is powerful but light and compact.

Grand Prix engines are built from the metals aluminum, magnesium, titanium and steel alloys. Aluminum is the most common material because it is light but strong.

Every Formula One car has a **turbocharged** engine. Turbocharging uses the energy of the engine's exhaust gases to spin a windmill-like pump. The pump forces large amounts of fuel and air into the engine's combustion chamber, where the fuel is burned. Turbocharging causes a greater quantity of fuel to be burned more quickly. This releases greater power and increases the car's speed. Turbochargers have been fitted to Formula One engines since the 1970s.

All Formula One cars have had rear-mounted engines since the 1960s. Drivers found that a car with the engine in the back was easier to handle.

↘ ACTION FACT

A Formula One engine can cost as much as $4 million to build.

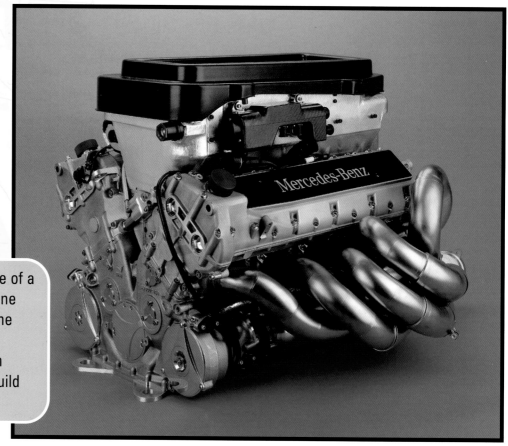

↗ The engine of a Formula One racing car. Engine designers use computer-driven robots to help build such engines.

SPONSORS AND LOGOS

The names of team **sponsors**, or their **logos**, are painted on the chassis. The position and size of the names and logos are carefully planned to give each car a distinctive look.

↘ **ACTION FACT**

It takes a Formula One car only 3.5 seconds to start, reach 100 miles (160 kilometers) per hour and stop.

The driver's gear

Helmets

Smooth surfaced, aerodynamically shaped helmets are worn to protect the driver, and to allow air to flow around and cool the head. Helmets must cover the driver's face and entire head. The visor, through which the driver sees, must be tough enough to withstand being hit by the stones that are thrown up from the track. These stones can hit the visor at up to 310 miles (500 kilometers) per hour. The visor has several see-through strips on it. When the top strip becomes dirty, the driver simply peels it off.

Helmets have a place where microphones and ear pieces can be attached. These devices enable the driver to communicate with mechanics in the pit. There is also a hole for a tube, which is attached to a supply of drinking water for the driver. It is important for the driver to replace the body fluid lost while driving the hot car. A driver can lose up to 6 cups (1.5 liters) of fluid during a race. Dehydration occurs when the body loses too much water, and it can cause the driver to lose concentration. A second tube, this one connected to a supply of air in case of an accident, can be attached to the helmet.

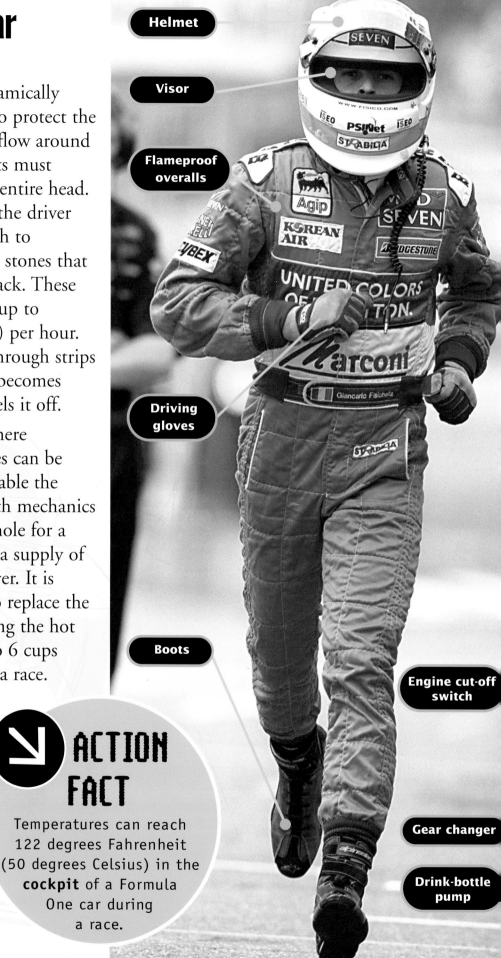

Helmet

Visor

Flameproof overalls

Driving gloves

Boots

Engine cut-off switch

Gear changer

Drink-bottle pump

↘ ACTION FACT

Temperatures can reach 122 degrees Fahrenheit (50 degrees Celsius) in the **cockpit** of a Formula One car during a race.

Flameproof clothing

Driving overalls are made of flameproof material. They can protect a driver from a fire for up to 12 seconds, which is usually enough time to leap out of a burning car. A long-sleeved T-shirt, long johns (underpants with long legs), socks and a balaclava, or head covering, make up the driver's underwear.

Driving gloves and boots

Gloves and boots are also made of flameproof material.

Onboard driver aids

A Formula One driver's job is made easier and safer with the use of driver aids in the car's cockpit. These include:

- computer-operated traction control – a device that calculates if a wheel is spinning too fast and adjusts it to improve traction and keep the car on the track
- semi-automatic gearbox – the gear change and clutch are hand-operated so the feet can be used solely for the accelerator and the brake.

The driver's overalls and underclothes are made of flameproof material.

ACTION FACT

A cooling vest, made of bubble-wrap plastic and filled with water to keep the driver cool during a race, was invented and tested in Australia in 2001.

ACTION FACT

Before helmet microphones were developed, the pit teams communicated with their drivers by writing messages on boards hung over the side of the pit wall. Drivers had to read the messages as they sped past the pit.

THE COCKPIT

Display for gears, engine revs, and water and oil temperatures

Lap time displays

Rev shift lights

Neutral gear button

Pit lane speed limiter

Pit-to-car radio activator

Changes menu on display

Brake balance selector

Electronic throttle regulator

Power-steering servo regulator

Selection 'enter' key

Manual activation of fuel door

Air/fuel mix selector

Specific car-program recall

Engine mapping selector

SKILLS, TRICKS AND TECHNIQUES

The set-up

The set-up involves adjusting the car so that it is well balanced, has a good grip in the corners of the track, and is capable of reaching high speeds down the **straight**. The set-up is the task of the race engineer. Using computers to run **simulated** laps, and taking into account the weather and other conditions of the track, the race engineer will plan the set-up. Mechanics then adjust the engine, wheels, car height and the aerofoil wings to make the car fit the set-up. Changes to the set-up can be made during and after qualifying races.

Qualifying laps

On the day before the Grand Prix, each driver has 12 laps in which to record their best time. The driver with the fastest lap time will take the **pole position** on the starting **grid** for the big race.

Planning strategies

Planning how a race will be run is called strategy. It involves deciding how much fuel the car will carry, how many **pit stops** to make and when to make them, which tires will be fitted to the car and when they will be changed. The team manager plans the race strategy with the other members of the team, including the driver.

Cars line up on the starting grid.

Grid positions

The grid determines how the cars line up for the start of the race. There are two cars per row on the grid with 26 feet (8 meters) between the rows.

The formation (warm-up) lap

Before the race begins, the drivers make a lap of the circuit. This is called the formation lap. They weave from side to side along the track to warm up the cars' tires. The brakes are applied hard because they too must be warmed up to work well. At the end of the formation lap, the drivers return to their grid positions for the start of the race.

The start

There are five red lights mounted across the track. The lights come on one at a time as the drivers line up on the grid. When all five lights are lit and then go out – all at the same time – the race begins.

Jockeying for position

Drivers rev their high-performance engines then release the clutch to transfer all the engine's power to the wheels for a fast and powerful start. The driver in pole position aims to maintain the lead and block any other driver from overtaking.

All drivers aim to overtake any cars in front of them, and all drivers aim to block those who are behind them. It is in the first few seconds of a race that drivers fight hardest to overtake slower cars. This can be a dangerous time as drivers battle to improve their positions in the field. As the race proceeds and the cars spread out, overtaking becomes less dangerous.

ACTION FACT

In the past, the start of a race was signaled by an official waving the flag of the country hosting the Grand Prix.

STARTING LIGHTS

Formula One racing is a dangerous sport. The risk of a multiple-car accident is greatest just seconds after the start of a race, at the first **chicane**. The drivers are not prepared to slow down much in case they are overtaken.

THE FORMULA ONE RACING
SCENE

Changing strategies

The most important decision to be made by each team during a Grand Prix race is how many refueling stops to make. A car carrying less fuel may travel faster because it is lighter. However, the car will have to make extra pit stops and possibly lose time at an important stage in the race. A car that is heavy with fuel will be able to stay on the track longer, but will be more easily overtaken by a car made lighter because it carries less fuel. Drivers, engineers and senior mechanics all help shape their team's racing strategy.

A team's strategy changes during the race in response to changing conditions on the track. If it begins to rain during a race, the team may decide to change to wet weather tires. These have deeper grooves and give a better grip on a wet track. This decision may mean making a longer pit stop than was planned, or even an extra stop.

Michael Schumacher discusses strategy with senior members of his team.

Driver fitness

Drivers in Formula One competitions must be physically fit. The **acceleration** and **deceleration** in a Formula One car places great strain on a driver's body. The driver is knocked about inside the car as it races around the bends and extreme corners of the track. Neck and back muscles must be strong to cope with the forces placed on them during a race. Inside the car, the temperature can reach 122 degrees Fahrenheit (50 degrees Celsius) and drivers lose body fluids rapidly. This can lead to dehydration, muscle cramps and a loss of concentration. These are dangerous conditions for a driver in control of a car traveling at more than 124 miles (200 kilometers) per hour.

Turning the steering wheel at high speeds takes strength. Drivers have said that when they round corners during a race, they feel like they're being hit on the back of the head with a hammer. The driver's job is painful, often frightening and very uncomfortable.

Jogging, cycling and working out in a gym are how drivers become and stay fit. Personal trainers plan a program of exercises to build stamina, strength and concentration. Trainers also supervise what the drivers eat. A nutritious diet is an important part of staying fit.

↗ A driver bends over in tiredness after a race.

↘ **ACTION FACT**

The forces on a driver's body during a Grand Prix race are almost the same as those on a fighter pilot.

↖ Staying fit gives Michael Schumacher the stamina and strength needed to compete in Formula One races.

15

In the pits

To make a pit stop, the driver exits the track and enters the pit using the **pit lane**. Speed in the pit lane is limited to 37 miles (60 kilometers) per hour. The driver must brake and stop in exactly the right spot in the pit so that no time is wasted.

About 20 mechanics work in the pit, organized in teams. The car-jack teams work to lift the vehicle so that the wheel-removal teams can replace each of the tires. Other mechanics refuel the car while one stands by with a fire extinguisher. A check is made of the car's air intakes and someone cleans the driver's visor. The chief mechanic oversees all the work and holds the stop board, known as a lollipop. This tells the driver when to enter and leave the pit.

All this activity takes place in about seven seconds, before the driver speeds off along the pit lane to rejoin the race.

No time to waste! Pit stops last only a few seconds. Mechanics work quickly in the pit, changing tires and refueling the car.

Practicing in the pits

Every second counts in a pit stop, so the pit crew must practice the pit stop procedures. Before spectators arrive for the big race, a car is wheeled into the pit in exactly the right spot. Then all the mechanics do their assigned jobs. They practice their tasks over and over again, trying to become the fastest pit team on the circuit.

Safety in the pits

The mechanics who work in the pit all wear flameproof overalls, gloves and helmets. Fire extinguishers are kept handy during refueling. A fuel pump is used with a special handle that cuts off the flow of fuel in an emergency. Refuelers wear breathing apparatus under their helmets. It is dangerous work.

ACTION FACT

Pit stops used to be allowed only in emergencies. In 1957 they became stops for tire changes only. They were not used for refueling until 1993.

Accidents during pit stops have claimed the lives of many people.

RACING SAFELY

Wheel cables

Wheels flying off a car during a race have always been a major safety hazard. Since 2001, it has been compulsory for Formula One cars to have two cables attached to each of the wheels.

↗ The two wheel cables help prevent the wheel from flying into the crowd or injuring other drivers on the track.

The safety car

The safety car is a road car with revolving lights. It is driven by an experienced circuit driver and carries an FIA official who can recognize all the competing cars. There is radio contact between the safety car and race control. Before the race starts, the safety car leads all the Formula One cars onto the track for one warm-up lap of the circuit before returning to the starting grid.

The safety car comes onto the track during a race when competitors or officials are in danger but the situation is not dangerous enough to stop the race.

TIRES WITH FOUR GROOVES

↖ The number of grooves in a tire affects the speed of a car. Since 1999, all tires fitted to Formula One cars must have four grooves to reduce speed and improve safety. Special tires are used for wet weather driving.

Yellow flags and a board with the letters 'SC' are displayed around the track to warn drivers that the safety car is on the track. All the competing cars must form a single line, in race order, behind the safety car. Overtaking is forbidden. The race leader must keep within five car lengths of the safety car.

When the clerk of the course decides that the danger has passed, the safety car is called in. It pulls into the pit lane and a green light signals that drivers can pick up speed again. The laps completed behind the safety car are counted as part of the race.

The racing cars line up behind the safety car.

Track safety

Near the bends in the circuit are sections of track covered with gravel. These gravel traps, nicknamed kitty-litter, are designed to rapidly slow down a car if it leaves the track. Flat run-off areas are also available around the track for drivers who have lost control of their cars and need to leave the track.

Gravel traps help to quickly slow down a car.

Protection for spectators

Metal barriers that allow a car to slide along them and tire barriers are good at stopping a speeding car and protecting spectators.

Tire barriers help to stop a speeding car.

Flags for safety

To keep the race as safe as possible, Formula One drivers must be kept informed about what is happening in the race. Race officials, called marshals, use flags to inform drivers about conditions on the track and events that may affect the drivers' safety. Each flag has a different meaning.

Any cars that have been overtaken by a lap of the circuit are not allowed to impede the progress of the faster cars. A blue flag is waved at the drivers of the slower cars when the lead cars have overtaken them.

- A blue flag tells the driver of the slower car to let the lead drivers pass quickly and safely. If a **backmarker** fails to move over after seeing a blue flag, the driver can be forced to stop in the pit for up to 10 seconds.

- A red flag signals that the race has had to be stopped before the finish.

- A yellow flag, when held still, signals that there is danger ahead and that overtaking is not allowed. A waved yellow flag instructs the driver to slow down and be ready to stop if necessary.

- The yellow flag and a board with the letters 'SC' are displayed around the track to warn drivers that the safety car is on the track. All competing cars must form a single line behind the safety car, in race order.

↗ After a crash on the circuit, the yellow flag is waved as a safety car leads the pack.

- A green flag signals that the danger is over and that overtaking is allowed again.
- A red-and-yellow striped flag signals that the track ahead is slippery. It may mean that oil has spilled onto the track surface.
- A black flag, together with an orange disc and a board containing the car's race number, signal that the car has a mechanical problem and must pull into the pit stop.
- A flag with white and black triangles, together with a board containing the car's race number, warn that the driver has been seen behaving in an unsporting way.
- A black flag, together with a board showing a car's race number, usually signal that the driver has been ordered to withdraw from the race and must return to the pit immediately.
- A white flag tells a driver that there is one lap remaining before the end of the race.
- A black-and-white checkered flag signals that the race is over.

The race is over when the black-and-white checkered flag is waved.

GRAND PRIX
RACING

Rules of the competition

- A Grand Prix race is held over a distance of at least 305 kilometers (190 miles) depending on the track or, if there are delays in the race, must last no more than two hours.
- The winner is the first driver to cover the distance.
- Points are awarded to the first six drivers who finish the race. There are 10 points for the winner, six points for second place, four points for third place, three points for fourth place, two points for fifth place and one point for sixth place. The driver with the most points at the end of the Grand Prix season wins the Driver's World Championship.
- Points are also awarded in the same way to the teams of the winning driver. The team with the most points at the end of the Grand Prix season wins the Constructor's Cup.
- Drivers are penalized if they break any rules such as jumping the start, blocking drivers who are about to lap them, or speeding in the pit lane. The penalty is usually an order to return to the pit for 10 seconds before rejoining the race.

The podium ceremony

The drivers who finish the race in first, second and third positions must attend the prize-giving ceremony on the podium immediately after the race. Standing on the podium, the drivers receive their prizes while the national anthem of the winner's country is played.

The Constructor's Cup is also awarded to the team that built the winning car. The national anthem of the team's country is played during the ceremony.

↗ FIA officials begin their inspection of a car to ensure it meets the Formula One rules.

At the podium ceremony, Mika Hakkinen raises his arms in triumph after winning the British Grand Prix in 2001.

Grand Prix Formula One circuits

Australian Grand Prix

Melbourne, Australia

- Track: 5.303 kilometers
- Length of race: 57 laps

Brazilian Grand Prix

Sao Paulo, Brazil

- Track: 4.292 kilometers
- Length of race: 72 laps

San Marino Grand Prix

Imola, San Marino

- Track: 4.929 kilometers
- Length of race: 62 laps

Monaco Grand Prix

Monte Carlo, Monaco

- Track: 3.366 kilometers
- Length of race: 78 laps

Spanish Grand Prix

Barcelona, Spain

- Track: 4.728 kilometers
- Length of race: 65 laps

Canadian Grand Prix

Montreal, Canada

- Track: 4.421 kilometers
- Length of race: 69 laps

French Grand Prix

Magny Cours, France

- Track: 4.247 kilometers
- Length of race: 72 laps

British Grand Prix

Silverstone, England

- Track: 5.137 kilometers
- Length of race: 60 laps

Austrian Grand Prix

A-1 Ring, Austria

- Track: 4.319 kilometers
- Length of race: 71 laps

German Grand Prix

Hockenheim, Germany

- Track: 6.822 kilometers
- Length of race: 45 laps

Hungarian Grand Prix

Hungaroring, Hungary

- Track: 3.972 kilometers
- Length of race: 77 laps

Belgian Grand Prix

Spa-Francorchamps, Belgium

- Track: 6.968 kilometers
- Length of race: 44 laps

Italian Grand Prix

Monza, Italy

- Track: 5.769 kilometers
- Length of race: 53 laps

European Grand Prix

Nurburgring, Luxembourg

- Track: 4.556 kilometers
- Length of race: 66 laps

Malaysian Grand Prix

Sepang, Malaysia

- Track: 5.542 kilometers
- Length of race: 56 laps

Japanese Grand Prix

Suzuka, Japan

- Track: 5.864 kilometers
- Length of race: 53 laps

The Formula One circuit at Hungaroring, Hungary.

Getting to the race venue

The lead-up to any Formula One event is a frantically busy time for the team. All the equipment and people have to be transported to the circuit in plenty of time for preparations to be made. Across Europe, enormous race trucks carry the team's cars and the workshop equipment to the track. Fuel trucks and huge motor homes join the race trucks on their journey. For Grand Prix events outside Europe, all the equipment and the people are transported by air.

↗ Motor homes are used as kitchens, dining rooms and offices for the team during the Grand Prix.

↘ On the big day, thousands of spectators crowd the side of the track for all the excitement of the Grand Prix.

GRAND PRIX CHAMPIONS

The top Formula One drivers come from many countries including Germany, Italy, Scotland, Finland and Brazil. Many of them began their driving careers in go-carts or the less-powerful Formula 3 cars before graduating to Formula One Grand Prix racing.

↗ Michael Schumacher

- Born January 3, 1969 in Germany
- Lives in Switzerland

Career highlights

- At age 16, runner-up in the go-kart racing Junior World Championships
- At age 18, go-kart racing European Champion
- In 1990, German Formula 3 Champion
- In 1991, made Grand Prix debut at the Belgian Grand Prix
- In 1994, Formula One World Champion
- In 1995, Formula One World Champion
- In 1999, driving for Ferrari; had his first serious accident and had to withdraw from the championship for six Grand Prix races
- In 2000, Formula One World Champion

Statistics:

- Grand Prix starts: 144
- Grand Prix wins: 45
- Qualified for pole position: 33 times

↗ David Coulthard

- Nicknamed 'The Flying Scotsman'
- Born March 27, 1971 in Scotland
- Lives in Monte Carlo, Monaco

Career highlights

- In 1982, had his first race in a go-kart at 11 years of age
- 1983–1985, Scottish Junior Kart Champion
- 1986–1987, Scottish Open and British Super 1 Kart Champion
- In 1989, McLaren/Autosport Young Driver of the Year
- 1991–1993, drove in Formula 3 competitions
- In 1994, Grand Prix Debut in Barcelona, Spain
- In 1998, third in Formula One World Championship

Statistics

- Grand Prix starts: 108
- Grand Prix wins: 9
- Qualified for pole position: 10 times

↗ Mika Hakkinen

- Nicknamed 'The Flying Finn'
- Born September 28, 1968 in Finland
- Lives in Monaco

Career highlights

- In 1975, won his first go-kart race at the age of seven
- 1981–1986, won the Finnish Karting Championships
- In 1987, first place Finnish, Swedish and Nordic Formula Ford 1600 Championships
- In 1990, first place British Formula 3 Championship
- In 1991, drove in his first Formula One Grand Prix race in Phoenix, Arizona
- In 1995, a serious accident during practice at the Australian Grand Prix resulted in severe head injuries; out of racing until 1997
- In 1998, Formula One World Champion
- In 1999, Formula One World Champion

Statistics

- Grand Prix starts: 146
- Grand Prix wins: 18
- Qualified for pole position: 26 times

↗ Jacques Villeneuve

- Born April 9, 1971 in Canada
- Lives in Monaco

Career highlights

- 1989–1993, drove in Formula 3 competitions
- In 1994, finished second at the Indy 500
- In 1995, won the Indy 500 and was named Indy-Car Champion Driver
- In 1996, drove in the Formula One Grand Prix race in Melbourne, Australia
- In 1997, Formula One World Champion

Statistics

- Grand Prix starts: 82
- Grand Prix wins: 11
- Qualified for pole position: 13 times

1894	1904	1906	1911	1920s	1947	1950
First car race in France was held on public roads.	Federation Internationale de l'Automobile (FIA) was formed and introduced rules to govern racing.	First ever Grand Prix was held on a closed-off road in Le Mans, France.	First Indy 500 race was held in the United States.	First single-seater cars were used in motor car racing.	First Grand Prix was held after the two world wars.	The beginning of the Formula One Championship: a fixed program of races by cars fitting the formula and racing according to the rules of the organizer.

1906

1920s

1950

1950–1960	1960s	1961	1968	1970s	1980s	1998
Indy 500 became part of the Formula One Championship. It was a 500-mile (804-kilometer) race held on the Indianapolis Motor Speedway in the United States.	Improvements were made to the design of racing cars, circuits and protective clothing for drivers, to cut the number of driver deaths.	Rear engines were required on all Formula One cars.	Aerofoil wings were added to Formula One cars and sponsors began painting their names on the cars. These foils were banned in 1969 after many broke off.	Improved aerodynamic design and the use of turbocharged engines made cars faster. **Ground effect technology** was introduced. Ground effects were banned in 1983 because speeds had become too great and unsafe.	Carbon fiber was used to build car chassis that were lighter and stronger.	Grooved tires were introduced to cut speed and improve safety. Improved safety measures including wheel cables were introduced.

1968

1998

29

RELATED ACTION
SPORTS

Formula One car racing is not the only type of race for single-driver cars. There are also Formula 3000 and Formula 3 races.

The FIA International Formula 3000 Championship

The F3000 is held each year on the same circuits as the Formula One car races. Started in 1985, the championship is seen as a stepping stone to Formula One. Current Formula One drivers Jean Alesi, David Coulthard and Rubens Barrichello all graduated from Formula 3000 into Formula One racing.

Formula 3000 follows most Formula One rules and regulations, with two major differences. In Formula 3000, all teams are supplied with two identical cars, and no refueling is allowed during a race.

↗ A Formula 3000 car.

Formula 3 racing

Formula 3 is a series of international car races held in England, Germany, Italy, France, Japan, Australia and South America.

Formula 3 cars look like scaled-down Grand Prix cars. They can reach speeds of up to 165 miles (265 kilometers) per hour. A Formula 3 chassis, known as the driver's tub, is constructed from many layers of carbon fiber matting placed over each other. An adhesive glues the layers together when the tub is baked in an oven. A carbon fiber chassis is stronger and lighter than one made of metal. Engine makers for Formula 3 cars include Toyota, Honda and Fiat.

If a Formula 3 car rolls over or is involved in a crash, the engine and gearbox will break away from the tub, protecting the driver from danger. The fuel tank also separates from the engine, reducing the risk of fire.

GLOSSARY

acceleration increase in speed

aerofoil wings wings shaped with curved surfaces that help reduce drag when traveling at high speeds

backmarker a slower car that is being overtaken by a lead car in a race

chassis the frame on which the car is built

chicane corners (narrow and winding sections of the track) included on the track to reduce the speed of cars and improve race safety

circuit a racetrack

cockpit the part of the car where the driver sits

Constructor's Cup an award given to the team which built the car that scores the most points by the end of the Grand Prix season

deceleration decrease in speed

grid area on the track where cars line up for the start of a race

ground effect technology a system that sucks air under the car, forcing the car down onto the track and improving grip and increasing speeds

logo a symbol representing a company

pit an area on the track where crews work on cars

pit lane a lane on the track reserved for cars entering or leaving the pit

pit stop a quick stop during a race for refueling, tire changing or repairs

pole position the front position on the starting grid

simulated when the racing conditions that exist on the track are recreated on computer so that different race strategies can be tested

sponsor a person or company that finances a Grand Prix team

straight the part of a race circuit track without curves

turbocharged describes an engine fitted with an exhaust-driven turbine to make it more powerful

INDEX

C

circuits 4, 24
clothes 11
cockpit 10, 11
construction 6–7
Constructor's Cup 7, 22
Coulthard, David 26

D

dehydration 10
driver aids 11
driver fitness 15
driver's gear 10–11

E

engine 5, 8

F

Federation Internationale de
    l'Automobile (FIA) 5, 22, 28
flags 20–1
formation lap 13
Formula 3 30
Formula 3000 30

G

grid 12

H

Hakkinen, Mika 27
helmets 10
history 4, 28–9

L

logos 9

M

mechanics 16–17

P

pits 10, 11, 16, 17
podium ceremony 22, 23
pole position 12, 13

Q

qualifying laps 12

R

rules 5, 22

S

safety 5, 10–11, 13, 17, 18–21
safety car 18–19
Schumacher, Michael 26
set-up 12
sponsors 9
strategy 12, 13–14

T

tires 18

V

Villeneuve, Jacques 27

W

wheel cables 5, 18